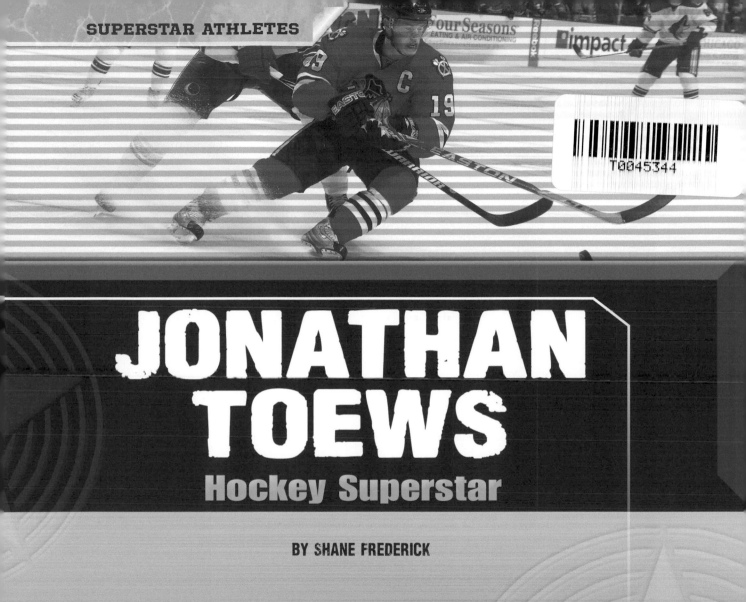

T0045344

JONATHAN TOEWS

Hockey Superstar

BY SHANE FREDERICK

CAPSTONE PRESS
a capstone imprint

Sports Illustrated KIDS

Sports Illustrated Kids Superstar Athletes are published by Capstone Press,
1710 Roe Crest Drive, North Mankato, Minnesota 56003.
www.capstonepub.com

Library of Congress Cataloging-in-Publication Data

Frederick, Shane.

Jonathan Toews : hockey superstar / by Shane Frederick.

pages cm.—(Sports illustrated kids. Superstar athletes.)

Includes bibliographical references and index.

Summary: "Introduces readers to the life of pro hockey star Jonathan Toews"—Provided by publisher.

ISBN 978-1-4765-9427-9 (library binding)

ISBN 978-1-4765-9432-3 (pbk.)

1. Toews, Jonathan, 1988– —Juvenile literature. 2. Hockey players—United States—Biography—Juvenile
literature. I. Title.

GV848.5.T64F74 2014

796.962092—dc23

[B]   2013034374

Editorial Credits

Nate LeBoutillier, editor; Lori Bye, designer; Eric Gohl, media researcher; Eric Manske, production specialist

Photo Credits

AP Photo: The Canadian Press/John Woods, 9; Courtesy of Shattuck-St. Mary's: 10; Newscom: UPI/Heinz
Ruckemann, 15; Sports Illustrated: Damian Strohmeyer, 12, David E. Klutho, cover (right), 1, 2–3, 5, 6, 16, 19, 21,
22 (all), Robert Beck, cover (left), 23, 24

Design Elements

Shutterstick/chudo-yudo, designerpix, Fassver Anna, Fazakas Mihaly

Direct Quotations

Page 6, from June 25, 2013, *Chicago Tribune* article "Toews Bounces Back from Injury to Play Starring Role" by
Colleen Kane, www.chicagotribune.com

Page 8, from March 8, 2013, *Splash Sun Times* article "Jonathan Toews: Ice Man" by Molly Each,
www.splash.suntimes.com

TABLE OF CONTENTS

CHAPTER 1

THE CAPTAIN RETURNS.............................. 4

CHAPTER 2

BORN TO PLAY HOCKEY 8

CHAPTER 3

A SERIOUS STAR 14

CHAPTER 4

WINNING WAYS 20

Timeline 22
Glossary 23
Read More 23
Internet Sites..24
Index..24

THE CAPTAIN RETURNS

Chicago Blackhawks **center** and **captain** Jonathan Toews had been roughed up. The Blackhawks were facing the Boston Bruins in the 2013 National Hockey League (NHL) Stanley Cup Finals. Bruised and battered, Toews was forced to watch the final period of Game 5 from the bench.

center—a skater whose main job is to play in the middle of the ice
captain—the player designated as the team leader; the captain wears the letter "C" on his jersey

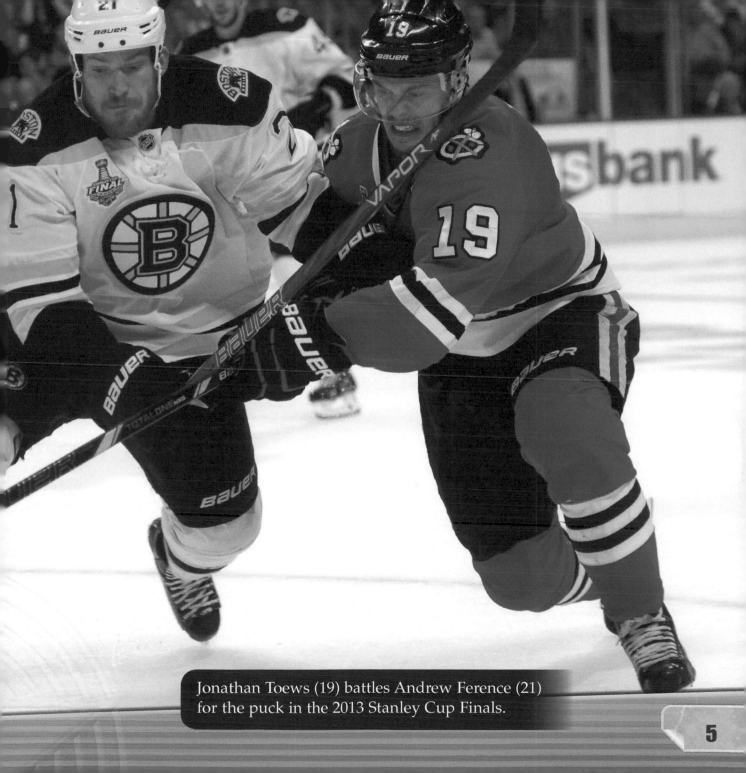

Jonathan Toews (19) battles Andrew Ference (21) for the puck in the 2013 Stanley Cup Finals.

Commisioner Gary Bettman hands off
the Stanley Cup to Jonathan Toews.

"There was no doubt in my mind I was going to find
a way to play tonight."
— Jonathan Toews after Game 6 of the
2013 Stanley Cup Finals

With the Blackhawks ahead three games to two, Toews returned to the ice for Game 6. In the second period, he snapped a quick shot through the legs of the Bruins' goalie. Still, the Bruins led 2-1 in the game's final moments. Then Toews floated a perfect pass to teammate Bryan Bickell for a goal. The goal tied the score and silenced the Boston crowd with 76 seconds left to play.

Moments later the Blackhawks scored again. As the game's final seconds ticked away, the celebration started. For the second time in four years, Toews and the Blackhawks were NHL champions.

CHAPTER 2

BORN TO PLAY HOCKEY

Hockey has always been a big part of Jonathan Toews' life. He grew up in Winnipeg, Manitoba, Canada, and began skating when he was just 3 years old. By the time he was 15, he was considered one of the best young players in North America.

"My dad made a backyard rink when we were growing up, and all the money my mom and dad made they pretty much spent sending us to hockey camp and buying us equipment. It was our life."
— Jonathan Toews

Jonathan Toews shows off the Stanley Cup to fans in his hometown of Winnipeg.

Toews moved to the United States to play high school hockey. He spent two years at Shattuck-St. Mary's in Minnesota, where NHL stars Sidney Crosby and Zach Parise played before him. During his senior year, Toews scored 110 **points** in 64 games and led the Sabres to a national championship.

point—a goal or an assist

After high school Toews played college hockey at the University of North Dakota. Toews helped UND earn back-to-back berths into the **Frozen Four**. He was named All-American after his second season. In 76 college games, he scored 40 goals and had 45 assists.

Frozen Four—the national semifinals and finals for college (NCAA) hockey

CHAPTER 3

A SERIOUS STAR

The Blackhawks selected Toews with the third overall pick in the 2006 **draft**. In 2007, after his sophomore year at North Dakota, Toews decided to turn pro. Just 19 years old, he scored a point in each of his first 10 NHL games. Toews went on to lead all rookies that season with 24 goals.

draft—an event in which professional teams choose new players

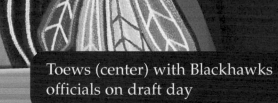

Toews (center) with Blackhawks officials on draft day

A season later the Blackhawks believed Toews was ready to be the team's leader. Though Toews was just 20 years old, they named him captain. He was the third-youngest NHL player ever to get a "C" stitched on his jersey. Toews was nicknamed "Captain Serious" by his teammates because he was so quiet and **mature** for his age.

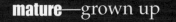
mature—grown up

In 2009–10 the Blackhawks had gone almost 50 years without winning a Stanley Cup. Toews led the charge to break that streak. He scored three game-winning goals and had 29 points in the playoffs as Chicago won the NHL championship. He was awarded the Conn Smythe Trophy as the most valuable player of the postseason. Three years later Toews was hoisting the Stanley Cup again.

INTERNATIONAL STAGE

Toews helped Canada capture the gold medal in the 2010 Winter Olympics. He also won gold medals representing his home country in the 2006 and 2007 World Junior Championships and the 2007 World Championships.

WINNING WAYS

Jonathan Toews was just the player the Chicago Blackhawks needed to start winning Stanley Cups again. His unique blend of offense, defense, and leadership helped the Blackhawks clinch two NHL championships. The fact that he did it so quickly may mean that there are even more titles to come.

A GREAT START

When Toews lifted the Stanley Cup for the second time, he accomplished something only the great Wayne Gretzky had done before him. Toews captained two championship teams by the time he was 25 years old.

TIMELINE

1988—Jonathan Toews is born April 29 in Winnipeg, Manitoba, Canada.

2005—Toews leads Minnesota's Shattuck-St. Mary's School to a USA Hockey national championship.

2006—The Chicago Blackhawks select Toews with the third overall pick in the NHL Draft.

2007—Toews leaves the University of North Dakota after two seasons to sign with the Blackhawks.

2008—The Blackhawks name Toews the team captain; he becomes the third-youngest captain in NHL history.

2010—Toews helps Team Canada capture the gold medal at the Winter Olympics in Vancouver; the Blackhawks defeat the Philadelphia Flyers to win the Stanley Cup as Toews is named playoff MVP.

2013—Toews leads the Blackhawks over the Boston Bruins for his second Stanley Cup championship.

GLOSSARY

captain (CAP-ten)—the player designated as the team leader; the captain wears the letter "C" on his jersey

center (SEN-ter)—a skater whose main job is to play in the middle of the ice

draft (DRAFT)—an event in which professional teams choose new players

Frozen Four (FRO-zen FORE)—the national semifinals and finals for college (NCAA) hockey

mature (ma-CHUR)—grown up

point (POINT)—a goal or an assist

READ MORE

Frederick, Shane. *The Ultimate Collection of Pro Hockey Records.* Sports Illustrated Kids. North Mankato, Minn.: Capstone Press, 2013.

Biskup, Agnieszka. *Hockey: How It Works.* Sports Illustrated Kids. North Mankato, Minn.: Capstone Press, 2010.

INTERNET SITES

FactHound offers a safe, fun way to find Internet sites related to this book. All of the sites on FactHound have been researched by our staff.

Here's all you do:

Visit *www.facthound.com*

Type in this code: 9781476594279

Super-cool stuff! Check out projects, games and lots more at **www.capstonekids.com**

INDEX

awards, 11, 13, 18, 22

Bickell, Bryan, 7

Boston Bruins, 4, 7, 22

Chicago Blackhawks, 4, 7, 14, 17, 18, 20, 22

Crosby, Sidney, 11

draft, 14, 22

Gretzky, Wayne, 20

Parise, Zach, 11

Shattuck-St. Mary's, 11, 22

Stanley Cup, 4, 6, 7, 18, 20, 22

Toews, Jonathan,
   childhood of, 8, 22
   high school career, 11, 22
   college career of, 13, 22
   international play, 18, 22

Winnipeg, Manitoba, Canada, 8, 22

University of North Dakota, 13, 14, 22